Shakespeare's Animals

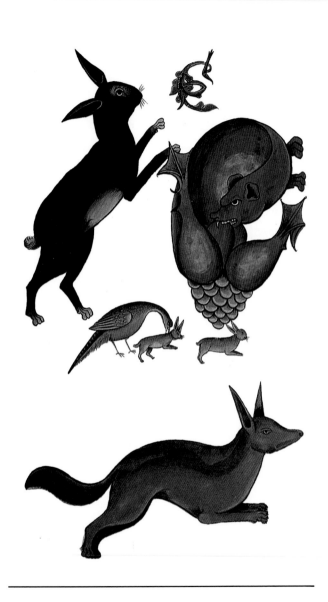

SHAKESPEARE'S
ANIMALS

PAVILION

First published in Great Britain in 1995 by
PAVILION BOOKS LIMITED
26 Upper Ground, London SE1 9PD

Text and pictures compiled by Jenny de Gex
Designed by David Fordham

A CIP catalogue record for this book is available from the
British Library.

ISBN 1 85793 571 3

Typeset by SX Composing Ltd in 9 on 11 Berling
Printed in China for Imago Publishing

2 4 6 8 10 9 7 5 3 1

This book may be ordered by post direct from the publisher.
Please contact the Marketing Department.
But try your bookshop first.

Contents

Introduction 7

The Ape 13
The Bear 14
The Birds 16
The Cat 17
The Cockatrice 20
The Crocodile 21
The Deer 22
The Dog 24
The Dolphin 28
The Dove 29
The Dragon 30
The Eagle 32
The Elephant 34
The Fox 36
The Goat 38

The Griffin 39
The Hart 40
The Hind 41
The Horse 42
The Lion 46
The Owl 48
The Panther 49
The Peacock 50
The Rabbit 51
The Ram 52
The Rat 54
The Stag 55
The Tiger 58
The Toad 60
The Unicorn 62

Picture Credits 64

ĲNTRODUCTION

SHAKESPEARE uses no fewer than 4,000 allusions to animals in his character portrayals, and so this small anthology can serve only as a brief appetiser to further riches in the tradition of comparing animal and human characteristics.

There are several realms within this tradition, the first being the supernatural, where animals are gods or demons, or weird metamorphosed creatures. The second realm is that of the *un*natural – the jointless elephant, the fire-eating salamander, the unlicked bear cub, and the basilisk or cockatrice, whose fatal eye brought certain death. The third realm is the analogy between man and animals.

The study of physiognomy judged men by the alleged attributes of the animals they supposedly resembled physically. Shakespeare may have known Della Porta's work *De Humana Physiogonomonia*, which was a compilation taken from Aristotle's *Historia Animalium*. *Aesop's Fables* would have been familiar to an Elizabethan audience, as the European edition was circulated in the fifteenth century. The Aesopic tradition, going back to earlier mythology (whether of Greek or Indian origin), represents another aspect of animal analogy, as the *Fables* tell of the follies and foibles of men depicted behind animal masks. Aesop was on the school curriculum in Elizabethan times, and probably no school child escaped the teaching of 'morality' by these picturesque examples. Ovid's *Metamorphoses*, with which Shakespeare would also have been familiar, is a storehouse of animal gods, auguries and charms, compiled from oral and written traditions originating with primitive peoples and passed on through the civilizations of Egypt, the Orient and Greece. Later books on witchcraft and magic continued these age-old folk beliefs.

Shakespeare was a countryman born and bred in Warwickshire, and his first-hand observations of nature form strong elements throughout his plays and poetry. The changing moods of the seasons echo romance or tragedy; bird songs convey blissful harmony or act as dire warnings; creatures act as symbols or premonitions of evil deeds.

Although Shakespeare would have recognized domestic and farm animals, and hunted or indeed poached wild deer, he would only ever have known the more exotic animals from the limited knowledge available in the late sixteenth century, for he would have had no opportunity of observing them in their wild and natural state. A strange lore grew out of man's interest in animals as marvellous specimens of nature. Travellers' tales, such as Hakluyt's voyages or Marco Polo's earlier journeys, filled the imagination long before the advent of the more exact science of zoology. Not all the tales of monsters were entirely without foundation, and as the world became better known, their existence was proven by eye-witness accounts and drawings, or by skins and bones brought back from distant lands.

Legends of dragons, mermaids and unicorns abounded and were repeated in the few early encylopaedic works before the advent of scientific proof. None more so than that of the unicorn, whose horn was imbued with miraculous properties. Even though we now know that the horn comes from a small Arctic whale, the narwhal, its associations conjure up a strangely magical world. The origins of the myth are

complex and buried deep in history: the unicorn's horn was
once a pagan symbol of male fertility, but was later purified
by the Christian church as a symbol of the Virgin's mystic
impregnation.

Strange beliefs about animals were disseminated in works
such as the first encyclopaedia, *De Proprietatibus Rerum* (Of
the Properties of Things), written by Bartholomaeus Angli-
cus in the thirteenth century, and in the works of Albertus
Magnus. The *Hortus Sanitatis* (or Medieval Health Hand-
book), famous for its herb lore, has a section on animal lore.
Classical literature in translation, such as Pliny's *Historia
Naturalis*, would also have been known to Shakespeare.
Extraordinary remedies are described – for instance, 'the
soles of the feet anointed with the fat of a Dormouse doth
procure sleep.' So it is not a great leap from this to the
strange concoctions of the witches' terrible brew in *Macbeth*,
for magic and folklore were integral parts of everyday life.

Shakespeare combined these elements, stories from the
classics, travel yarns, folklore, magic, childhood memories
and heraldry, and used the old technique of animal analogy
more extensively than any previous epic writers, dramatists
or poets. Homer pictured warriors fighting like lions, boars
and fierce bulls in the ferocity of war, and Shakespeare fol-
lowed this technique.

Animal comparisons range from the bee to the lion, the
former in a detailed description of an ideal kingdom
modelled after the government of bees (*King Henry V*, Act I,
Scene II); the latter, the 'king of beasts' in many of the
history plays, where the English lion is at war with the
French. The comparisons, used in so many different contexts
– be they political, heroic, farcical, tragic, romantic or bla-
tantly sexual – often typified the disposition, rather than
appearance, of a character. Frequently they were used with
hostile intent, as in metaphors of battle and treachery, or for
censure or ridicule, in the case of villains (such as Richard III

Elephas hic per Europam vifus eft
Anno 1629

or Shylock) and buffoons (such as Dogberry or Bottom). Richard III, whose brutish nature retains a certain majesty, is characterized as wolf, spider, tiger, boar and bloody dog. Armies rallied against 'the wretched, bloody and usurping boar', of whom it was said: 'never hung poison on a fouler toad'. His birth was heralded thus:

> *A cockatrice hast thou hatch'd to the world,*
> *Whose unavoided eye is murderous!*

Specific animals, such as the serpent, the fox and the wolf are associated with treachery and villainy. This can vary according to the context – a lion may alternately be cruel and merciful, an ape sensual and ludicrous. The word 'serpent' applied to Goneril means treacherous, as she struck 'with her tongue, most serpent-like upon the very heart' (both she and Richard III are described as 'gilded serpents'), but when applied to Cleopatra it means alluring and sensuous, Antony's 'serpent of old Nile'.

Gentler creatures like the lamb, dove, hare and birds convey expressions of love and friendship, or serve as innocent victims, as for Katherine in *The Taming of the Shrew*: 'Tut! She's a lamb, a dove, a fool to him.' One of the most pitiful speeches from *Macbeth* comes when Macduff hears with horror of the murder of his wife and children:

> *What! all my pretty chickens and their dam*
> *At one fell swoop?*

And Sir Andrew Aguecheek, one of the greatest fools in all Shakespeare's work, is compared to witless animals, for his 'dormouse valour' and having 'not so much blood in his liver as will clog the foot of a flea'.

Names are frequently used for the sake of word-play – deer and dear, hart and heart – or for the double meaning and innuendo conveyed by certain creatures. The Elizabethans had a bawdy sense of humour, and many of the animal interpretations had a sexual meaning that is lost from our current language. Where men and women abandon themselves to passion, they become beasts. Thus in *Othello*, Iago describes how 'your daughter and the Moor are now making the beast with two backs'. Although an ass was also a general term of abuse, and Dogberry a quite natural ass, its other meaning was not lost on Shakespearean audiences.

Like Aesop, Shakespeare often adopted a moral tone and does not merely give us narrative: instead, he puts a moral or political lesson into the words of his characters. In his portrayal of Mankind, he often makes sweeping generalizations, turning to the animal kingdom for comparisons. He satirizes or praises where appropriate the weak, villainous, pathetic or heroic. The metamorphosis of man into animal often retains a human soul. In the words of Hamlet:

11

> *What a piece of work is a man! How noble in*
> *reason! how infinite in faculty! in form and moving*
> *how express and admirable! in action how like an*
> *angel! in apprehension how like a god! the beauty*
> *of the world! the paragon of animals!*

Elizabethan staging, which used partial disguise of men as animals, was violently condemned for 'metamorphosing humane shape into bestiall forme'! Many supernatural animal figures move across the Elizabethan stage: satyrs, harpies, animal familiars. The strangest, part-animal supernatural figure is Caliban – 'a freckled whelp, hag-born'.

> *What have we here? a man or a fish?*
> *Half a fish and half a monster.*

The illustrations for this anthology form part of a pattern book dating from the early Tudor period, of uncertain origin but similar to a rare contemporary manuscript from Suffolk now in the Mellon Collection, known as the *Helmingham Herbal and Bestiary*. Both works give a unique view of daily life at the turn of the fifteenth century, and two strands can be traced, as with Shakespeare: the moralistic, represented by the bestiary; and the informative, mainly about hunting. Legendary nature influenced the drawings, as did the stylization of the new discipline of heraldry. The manuscripts may have been patterns for textiles or embroidery.

The Elizabethans would have been closer to the Aesopic traditions and to those of animal physiognomy than we are today, but through Shakespeare's interpretations and character portrayals we are made to see Man's fundamental sensuality, stupidity and cruelty. Our passions and behaviour, at a basic level, are similar to those of all other animals. It is only through the refinements of our civilization, such as the richness of Shakespeare's language which has endured for nearly 400 years, that we can rise above these baser instincts.

⟨THE APE

ACT II   SCENE I

Oberon:

Having once this juice,
I'll watch Titania when she is asleep,
And drop the liquor of it in her eyes:
The next thing then she waking looks upon,
(Be it on lion, bear, or wolf, or bull,
On meddling monkey, or on busy ape,)
She shall pursue it with the soul of love.
And ere I take this charm off from her sight,
(As I can take it, with another herb,)
I'll make her render up her page to me.
But who comes here? I am invisible;
And I will overhear their conference.

THE BEAR

KING LEAR

ACT III   SCENE IV

Lear:

Thou think'st 'tis much, that this contentious storm
Invades us to the skin: so 'tis to thee;
But where the greater malady is fix'd,
The lesser is scarce felt. Thou'dst shun a bear:
But if thy flight lay toward the roaring sea,
Thou'dst meet the bear i' the mouth. When the
    mind's free,
The body's delicate: the tempest in my mind
Doth from my senses take all feeling else,
Save what beats there. – Filial ingratitude!
Is it not as this mouth should tear this hand,
For lifting food to't? – But I will punish home: –
No, I will weep no more. – In such a night
To shut me out! – Pour on; I will endure: –
In such a night as this! O Regan, Goneril! –
Your old kind father, whose frank heart gave all, –
O, that way madness lies; let me shun that;
No more of that. –

THE BEAR

A MIDSUMMER NIGHT'S DREAM

ACT II   SCENE II

Oberon:

What thou see'st, when thou dost wake,
(*Squeezes the flower on* TITANIA's *eyelids*)
Do it for thy true-love take;
Love and languish for his sake;
Be it ounce, or cat, or bear,
Pard, or boar with bristled hair,
In thy eye that shall appear
When thou wak'st, it is thy dear;
Wake, when some vile thing is near.

THE BIRDS

'To see his face the lion walk'd along
  Behind some hedge, because he would not fear him;
  To recreate himself, when he hath sung,
  The tiger would be tame, and gently hear him;
    If he had spoke, the wolf would leave his prey,
    And never fright the silly lamb that day.

'When he beheld his shadow in the brook,
  The fishes spread on it their golden gills;
  When he was by, the birds such pleasure took,
  That some would sing, some other in their bills
    Would bring him mulberries, and ripe-red
      cherries;
    He fed them with his sight, they him with
      berries.'

THE CAT

ACT III   GOWER

Gower:

Now sleep yslaked hath the rout;
No din but snores, the house about,
Made louder by the o'er-fed breast
Of this most pompous marriage-feast,
The cat, with eyne of burning coal,
Now couches from the mouse's hole;
And crickets sing at the oven's mouth,
Aye the blither for their drouth.
Hymen hath brought the bride to bed,
Where, by the loss of maidenhead,
A babe is moulded. – Be attent,
And time that is so briefly spent,
With your fine fancies quaintly eche;
What's dumb in show, I'll plain with speech.

THE CAT

ACT IV   SCENE I

First Witch:

Thrice the brinded cat hath mew'd.
Second Witch: Thrice; and once the hedge-pig
    whined.
Third Witch: Harpier cries: – 'tis time, 'tis time.
First Witch: Round about the cauldron go;
In the poison'd entrails throw.

Toad, that under cold stone,
Days and nights hast thirty-one,
Swelter'd venom sleeping got,
Boil thou first i' the charmed pot!
All: Double, double toil and trouble;
Fire, burn; and, cauldron, bubble.
Second Witch: Fillet of a fenny snake,
In the cauldron boil and bake:
Eye of newt, and toe of frog,
Wool of bat, and tongue of dog,
Adder's fork, and blind-worm's sting,
Lizard's leg, and owlet's wing,
For a charm of powerful trouble,
Like a hell-broth boil and bubble.
All: Double, double toil and trouble;
Fire, burn; and, cauldron, bubble.
Third Witch: Scale of dragon, tooth of wolf;
Witches' mummy; maw, and gulf,
Of the ravin'd salt-sea shark;
Root of hemlock, digg'd i' the dark;
Liver of blaspheming Jew;
Gall of goat, and slips of yew,
Sliver'd in the moon's eclipse;
Nose of Turk, and Tartar's lips;
Finger of birth-strangled babe,
Ditch-deliver'd by a drab, –
Make the gruel thick and slab
Add thereto a tiger's chaudron,
For the ingredients of our cauldron.
All: Double, double toil and trouble;
Fire, burn; and, cauldron, bubble.
Second Witch: Cool it with a baboon's blood,
Then the charm is firm and good.

THE COCKATRICE

THE RAPE OF LUCRECE

Then, for thy husband and thy children's sake,
Tender my suit: bequeath not to their lot
The shame that from them no device can take,
The blemish that will never be forgot;
Worse than a slavish wipe, or birth-hour's blot:
  For marks descried in men's nativity
  Are nature's faults, not their own infamy.'

Here with a cockatrice' dead-killing eye
He rouseth up himself, and makes a pause;
While she, the picture of pure piety,
Like a white hind under the grype's sharp claws,
Pleads, in a wilderness, where are no laws,
  To the rough beast that knows no gentle right,
  Nor aught obeys but his foul appetite.

But when a black-faced cloud the world doth threat,
In his dim mist the aspiring mountains hiding,
From earth's dark womb some gentle gust doth get,
Which blows these pitchy vapours from their
      biding,
Hindering their present fall by this dividing;
  So his unhallow'd haste her words delays,
  And moody Pluto winks while Orpheus plays.

THE CROCODILE

ACT IV   SCENE I

Desdemona:

I have not deserved this.

Lodovico:

My lord, this would not be believed in Venice,
Though I should swear I saw't: 'tis very much;
Make her amends; she weeps.

Othello:

O devil, devil!
If that the earth could teem with woman's tears,
Each drop she falls would prove a crocodile: –
Out of my sight!

Desdemona:

I will not stay to offend you.

21

THE DEER

VENUS AND ADONIS

F ondling,' she saith, 'since I have hemm'd thee here,
Within the circuit of this ivory pale,
I'll be a park, and thou shalt be my deer;
Feed where thou wilt, on mountain or in dale:
Graze on my lips; and if those hills be dry,
Stray lower, where the pleasant fountains lie.

'Within this limit is relief enough,
Sweet bottom-grass, and high delightful plain,
Round rising hillocks, brakes obscure and rough,
To shelter thee from tempest and from rain;
Then be my deer, since I am such a park;
No dog shall rouse thee, though a thousand bark.'

THE DEER

VENUS AND ADONIS

And as she runs, the bushes in the way
  Some catch her by the neck, some kiss her face,
  Some twine about her thigh to make her stay;
  She wildly breaketh from their strict embrace,
    Like a milch doe, whose swelling dugs do ache,
    Hasting to feed her fawn hid in some brake.

By this, she hears the hounds are at a bay;
Whereat she starts, like one that spies an adder
Wreathed up in fatal folds, just in his way,
The fear whereof doth make him shake and
    shudder;
    Even so the timorous yelping of the hounds
    Appals her senses, and her spirit confounds.

For now she knows it is no gentle chase,
But the blunt boar, rough bear, or lion proud,
Because the cry remaineth in one place,
Where fearfully the dogs exlaim aloud:
    Finding their enemy to be so curst,
    They all strain court'sy who shall cope him first.

This dismal cry rings sadly in her ear,
Through which it enters to surprise her heart;
Who, overcome by doubt and bloodless fear,
With cold-pale weakness numbs each feeling part:
    Like soldiers, when their captain once doth yield,
    They basely fly, and dare not stay the field.

THE DOG

MACBETH

ACT III   SCENE I

First Murderer:

e are men, my liege.

Macbeth:

Ay, in the catalogue ye go for men;
As hounds, and greyhounds, mongrels, spaniels, curs,
Shoughs, water-rugs, and demi-wolves, are cleped
All by the name of dogs: the valued file
Distinguishes the swift, the slow, the subtle,
The housekeeper, the hunter, every one
According to the gift which bounteous nature
Hath in him closed; whereby he does receive
Particular addition, from the bill
That writes them all alike: and so of men.
Now, if you have a station in the file,
Not in the worst rank of manhood, say it;
And I will put that business in your bosoms
Whose execution takes your enemy off;
Grapples you to the heart and love of us,
Who wear our health but sickly in his life,
Which in his death were perfect.

𝒯HE DOG

ACT III   SCENE VI

Edgar:

Avaunt, you curs!
  Be thy mouth or black or white,
  Tooth that poisons if it bite;
  Mastiff, grey-hound, mongrel grim,
  Hound or spaniel, brach or lym;
  Or bobtail tike, or trundle-tail;
  Tom will make him weep and wail:
  For, with throwing thus my head,
  Dogs leap the hatch, and all are fled.

THE DOG

THE MERCHANT OF VENICE

ACT I   SCENE III

Shylock:

Signior Antonio, many a time and oft
In the Rialto you have rated me
About my moneys, and my usances:
Still have I borne it with a patient shrug;
For sufferance is the badge of all our tribe:
You call me misbeliever, cut-throat dog,
And spit upon my Jewish gaberdine,
And all for use of that which is mine own.
Well then, it now appears you need my help:
Go to, then: you come to me, and you say,
Shylock, we would have moneys; you say so;
You, that did void your rheum upon my beard,
And foot me, as you spurn a stranger cur
Over your threshold; moneys is your suit.
What should I say to you? Should I not say,
Hath a dog money? is it possible
A cur can lend three thousand ducats? or
Shall I bend low, and in a bondman's key,
With 'bated breath, and whispering humbleness,
Say this, —
Fair sir, you spet on me on Wednesday last;
You spurn'd me such a day; another time
You call'd me dog; and for these courtesies
I'll lend you thus much moneys?

THE DOG

ACT III   SCENE I

Antony:

O pardon me, thou bleeding piece of earth,
That I am meek and gentle with these butchers!
Thou are the ruins of the noblest man
That ever livèd in the tide of times.
Woe to the hand that shed this costly blood!
Over thy wounds now do I prophesy, –
Which, like dumb mouths, do ope their ruby lips,
To beg the voice and utterance of my tongue, –
A curse shall light upon the limbs of men;
Domestic fury, and fierce civil strife,
Shall cumber all the parts of Italy:
Blood and destruction shall be so in use,
And dreadful objects so familiar,
That mothers shall but smile when they behold
Their infants quarter'd with the hands of war;
All pity choked with custom of fell deeds:
And Caesar's spirit, ranging for revenge,
With Até by his side, come hot from hell,
Shall in these confines, with a monarch's voice,
Cry *Havoc*, and let slip the dogs of war;
That this foul deed shall smell above the earth
With carrion men, groaning for burial.

THE DOLPHIN

ANTONY AND CLEOPATRA

ACT V   SCENE II

Cleopatra:

His legs bestrid the ocean: his rear'd arm
Crested the world: his voice was propertied
As all the tunèd spheres, and that to friends;
But when he meant to quail and shake the orb,
He was as rattling thunder. For his bounty,
There was no winter in't: an autumn 'twas,
That grew the more by reaping: his delights
Were dolphin-like; they show'd his back above
The element they lived in: in his livery
Walk'd crowns and crownets; realms and islands were
As plates dropp'd from his pocket.

Dolabella:

Cleopatra, –

Cleopatra:

Think you there was, or might be, such a man
As this I dreamt of?

Dolabella:

Gentle madam, no.

Cleopatra:

You lie, up to the hearing of the gods.
But, if there be, or ever were, one such,
It's past the size of dreaming: Nature wants stuff
To vie strange forms with fancy; yet, to imagine
An Antony, were Nature's piece 'gainst fancy,
Condemning shadows quite.

THE DOVE

Witness this primrose bank whereon I lie;
These forceless flowers like sturdy trees support
me;
Two strengthless doves will draw me through
the sky,
From morn till night, even where I list to sport
me:
Is love so light, sweet boy, and may it be
That thou shouldst think it heavy unto thee?

'Is thine own heart to thine own face affected?
Can thy right hand seize love upon thy left?
Then woo thyself, be of thyself rejected,
Steal thine own freedom, and complain on
theft.
Narcissus so himself himself forsook,
And died to kiss his shadow in the brook.'

*T*HE DRAGON

ACT I   SCENE I

Bedford:

Hung be the heavens with black, yield day to night!
Comets, importing change of times and states,
Brandish your crystal tresses in the sky;
And with them scourge the bad revolting stars,
That have concented unto Henry's death!
King Henry the fifth, too famous to live long!
England ne'er lost a king of so much worth.

Gloucester:

England ne'er had a king until his time.
Virtue he had, deserving to command:
His brandish'd sword did blind men with his beams;
His arms spread wider than a dragon's wings:
His sparkling eyes, replete with wrathful fire,
More dazzled and drove back his enemies,
Than mid-day sun, fierce bent against their faces.
What should I say? his deeds exceed all speech:
He ne'er lift up his hand but conquered.

30

THE DRAGON

THE EAGLE

THE EAGLE

KING HENRY V

ACT I   SCENE II

Westmoreland:

B
ut there's a saying, very old and true, —

If that you will France win,
Then with Scotland first begin;

For once the eagle England being in prey,
To her unguarded nest the weasel Scot
Comes sneaking, and so sucks her princely eggs;
Playing the mouse, in absence of the cat,
To spoil and havoc more than she can eat.

Exeter:

It follows, then, the cat must stay at home:
Yet that is but a crush'd necessity;
Since we have locks to safeguard necessaries,
And pretty traps to catch the petty thieves.
While that the armed hand doth fight abroad,
The advisèd head defends itself at home:
For government, through high, and low, and lower,
Put into parts, doth keep in one concent;
Congreeing in a full and natural close,
Like music.

THE ELEPHANT

TROILUS AND CRESSIDA

ACT I   SCENE II

Alexander:

This man, lady, hath robbed many beasts of their particular additions; he is as valiant as the lion, churlish as the bear, slow as the elephant; a man into whom nature hath so crowded humours, that his valour is crushed into folly, his folly sauced with discretion: there is no man hath a virtue that he hath not a glimpse of; nor any man an attaint but he carries some stain of it: he is melancholy without cause, and merry against the hair: he hath the joints of everything, but everything so out of joint, that he is a gouty Briareus, many hands and no use; or purblinded Argus, all eyes and no sight.

Cressida:

But how should this man, that makes me smile, make Hector angry?

Alexander:

They say he yesterday coped Hector in the battle, and struck him down; the disdain and shame whereof hath ever since kept Hector fasting and waking.

THE ELEPHANT

THE FOX

KING LEAR

ACT V   SCENE III

Lear:

Upon such sacrifices, my Cordelia,
The gods themselves throw incense. Have I caught
        thee?
He that parts us shall bring a brand from heaven,
And fire us hence, like foxes. Wipe thine eyes;
The good years shall devour them, flesh and fell,
Ere they shall make us weep: we'll see them starve
        first.
Come.

THE FOX

ACT V   SCENE II

Worcester:

Then are we all undone.
It is not possible, it cannot be,
The king would keep his word in loving us:
He will suspect us still, and find a time
To punish this offence in other faults:
Suspicion, all our lives, shall be stuck full of eyes:
For treason is but trusted like the fox;
Who, ne'er so tame, so cherish'd, and lock'd up,
Will have a wild trick of his ancestors.
Look how we can, or sad, or merrily,
Interpretation will misquote our looks;
And we shall feed like oxen at a stall,
The better cherish'd still the nearer death.
My nephew's trespass may be well forgot,
It hath the excuse of youth, and heat of blood;
And an adopted name of privilege, –
A hare-brain'd Hotspur, govern'd by a spleen:
All his offences live upon my head,
And on his father's; – we did train him on;
And, his corruption being ta'en from us,
We, as the spring of all, shall pay for all.
Therefore, good cousin, let not Harry know,
In any case, the offer of the king.

THE GOAT

OTHELLO

ACT III   SCENE III

Othello:

Think'st thou, I'd make a life of jealousy,
To follow still the changes of the moon
With fresh suspicions? No: to be once in doubt,
Is once to be resolved. Exchange me for a goat,
When I shall turn the business of my soul
To such exsufflicate and blown surmises,
Matching thy inference. 'Tis not to make me jealous,
To say my wife is fair, feeds well, loves company,
Is free of speech, sings, plays, and dances;
Where virtue is, these are more virtuous:
Nor from mine own weak merits will I draw
The smallest fear, or doubt of her revolt;
For she had eyes, and chose me. No, Iago;
I'll see before I doubt: when I doubt, prove;
And, on the proof, there is no more but this,-
Away at once with love, or jealousy.

THE GRIFFIN

ACT III   SCENE I

Hotspur:

I cannot choose: sometime he angers me,
With telling me of the moldwarp and the ant,
Of the dreamer Merlin, and his prophecies;
And of a dragon and a finless fish,
A clip-wing'd griffin, and a moulten raven,
A couching lion, and a ramping cat,
And such a deal of skimble-skamble stuff
As puts me from my faith. I tell you what, –
He held me, last night, at least nine hours,
In reckoning up the several devils' names
That were his lackeys: I cried, *hum*, – and *well*, – go to, –
But mark'd him not a word. O, he's as tedious
As is a tired horse, a railing wife;
Worse than a smoky house: – I had rather live
With cheese and garlic in a windmill, far,
Than feed on cates, and have him talk to me,
In any summer-house in Christendom.

The Hart

JULIUS CAESAR

ACT III   SCENE I

Antony:

That I did love thee, Caesar, O, 'tis true:
If then thy spirit look upon us now,
Shall it not grieve thee, dearer than thy death,
To see thy Antony making his peace,
Shaking the bloody fingers of thy foes,
Most noble! in the presence of thy corse?
Had I as many eyes as thou hast wounds,
Weeping as fast as they stream forth thy blood,
It would become me better, than to close
In terms of friendship with thine enemies.
Pardon me, Julius! – Here wast thou bay'd, brave hart;
Here didst thou fall; and here thy hunters stand,
Sign'd in thy spoil, and crimson'd in thy lethe.
O world! thou wast the forest to this hart;
And this, indeed, O world! the heart of thee. –
How like a deer, stricken by many princes,
Dost thou here lie!

The Hind

AS YOU LIKE IT

ACT III   SCENE II

Touchstone:

If a hart do lack a hind,
Let him seek out Rosalind.
If the cat will after kind,
So, be sure, will Rosalind.
Winter-garments must be lined,
So must slender Rosalind.
They that reap must sheaf and bind;
Then to cart with Rosalind.
Sweetest nut hath sourest rind,
Such a nut is Rosalind.
He that sweetest rose will find,
Must find love's prick and Rosalind.

THE HORSE

VENUS AND ADONIS

His ears up prick'd; his braided hanging mane
Upon his compass'd crest now stand on end;
His nostrils drink the air, and forth again,
As from a furnace, vapours doth he send:
    His eye, which scornfully glisters like fire,
    Shows his hot courage and his high desire.

Sometimes he trots, as if he told the steps,
With gentle majesty, and modest pride;
Anon he rears upright, curvets, and leaps,
As who should say, Lo! thus my strength is tried;
    And this I do to captivate the eye
    Of the fair breeder that is standing by.

What recketh he his rider's angry stir,
His flattering 'holla,' or his 'Stand, I say'?
What cares he now for curb, or pricking spur?
For rich caparisons, or trapping gay?
    He sees his love, and nothing else he sees,
    Nor nothing else with his proud sight agrees.

Look, when a painter would surpass the life,
In limning out a well-proportion'd steed,
His art with nature's workmanship at strife,
As if the dead the living should exceed;
    So did this horse excel a common one,
    In shape, in courage, colour, pace, and bone.

THE HORSE

Round-hoof'd, short-jointed, fetlocks shag and long,
Broad breast, full eye, small head, and nostril wide,
High crest, short ears, straight legs, and passing
    strong,
Thin mane, thick tail, broad buttock, tender hide:
  Look, what a horse should have, he did not lack,
  Save a proud rider on so proud a back.

Sometime he scuds far off, and there he stares;
Anon he starts at stirring of a feather;
To bid the wind a base he now prepares,
And whether he run, or fly, they knew not whether;
  For through his mane and tail the high wind sings.
  Fanning the hairs, who wave like feather'd wings.

He looks upon his love, and neighs unto her;
She answers him, as if she knew his mind:
Being proud, as females are, to see him woo her,
She puts on outward strangeness, seems unkind;
  Spurns at his love, and scorns the heat he feels,
  Beating his kind embracements with her heels.

Then, like a melancholy malcontent,
He vails his tail, that, like a falling plume,
Cool shadow to his melting buttock lent;
He stamps, and bites the poor flies in his fume:
  His love, perceiving how he is enraged,
  Grew kinder, and his fury was assuaged.

THE HORSE

THE HORSE

SONNET LI

Thus can my love excuse the slow offence
Of my dull bearer, when from thee I speed:
From where thou art why should I haste me thence?
Till I return, of posting is no need.
O, what excuse will my poor beast then find,
When swift extremity can seem but slow?
Then should I spur, though mounted on the wind;
In winged speed no motion shall I know:
Then can no horse with my desire keep pace;
Therefore desire, of perfect'st love being made,
Shall neigh (no dull flesh) in his fiery race;
But love, for love, thus shall excuse my jade, –
　　Since from thee going he went wilful-slow,
　　Towards thee I'll run, and give him leave to go.

THE LION

TIMON OF ATHENS

ACT IV   SCENE III

Timon:

If thou wert the lion, the fox would beguile thee; if thou wert the lamb, the fox would eat thee: if thou wert the fox, the lion would suspect thee, when, peradventure, thou wert accused by the ass: if thou wert the ass, thy dulness would torment thee; and still thou livedst but as a breakfast to the wolf: if thou wert the wolf, thy greediness would afflict thee, and oft thou shouldst hazard thy life for thy dinner: wert thou the unicorn, pride and wrath would confound thee, and make thine own self the conquest of thy fury: wert thou a bear, thou wouldst be killed by the horse; wert thou a horse, thou wouldst be seized by the leopard: wert thou a leopard, thou wert german to the lion, and the spots of thy kindred were jurors on thy life: all thy safety were remotion; and thy defence, absence. What beast couldst thou be, that were not subject to a beast? and what a beast art thou already, that see'st not thy loss in transformation!

*T*HE LION

JULIUS CAESAR

ACT I   SCENE III

Cassius:

Y ou look pale, and gaze,
  And put on fear, and cast yourself in wonder,
  To see the strange impatience of the heavens:
But if you would consider the true cause
Why all these fires, why all these gliding ghosts,
Why birds and beasts, from quality and kind;
Why old men, fools, and children calculate;
Why all these things change from their ordinance,
Their natures, and pre-formed faculties,
To monstrous quality; – why, you shall find,
That heaven hath infused them with these spirits,
To make them instruments of fear and warning
Unto some monstrous state.
Now could I, Casca, name to thee a man
Most like this dreadful night;
That thunders, lightens, opens graves, and roars
As doth the lion in the Capitol;
A man no mightier than thyself, or me,
In personal action; yet prodigious grown,
And fearful, as these strange eruptions are.

Casca:

'Tis Caesar that you mean: is it not, Cassius?

THE OWL

VENUS AND ADONIS

Look, the world's comforter, with weary gait,
His day's hot task hath ended in the west:
The owl, night's herald, shrieks – 'tis very late;
The sheep are gone to fold, birds to their nest;
    And coal-black clouds that shadow heaven's light
    Do summon us to part, and bid good night.

'Now let me say "good night," and so say you;
If you will say so, you shall have a kiss.'
'Good night,' quoth she; and, ere he says 'adieu,'
The honey fee of parting tender'd is:
    Her arms do lend his neck a sweet embrace;
    Incorporate then they seem; face grows to face;

Tilll, breathless, he disjoin'd, and backward drew
The heavenly moisture, that sweet coral mouth,
Whose precious taste her thirsty lips well knew,
Whereon they surfeit, yet complain on drouth:
    He with her plenty press'd, she faint with dearth,
    (Their lips together glued,) fall to the earth.

THE PANTHER

TITUS ANDRONICUS

ACT II   SCENE II

Titus Andronicus:

The hunt is up, the morn is bright and gray,
The fields are fragrant, and the woods are green;
Uncouple here, and let us make a bay,
And wake the emperor and his lovely bride,
And rouse the prince, and ring a hunter's peal,
That all the court may echo with the noise.
Sons, let it be your charge, as it is ours,
To attend the emperor's person carefully:
I have been troubled in my sleep this night,
But dawning day new comfort hath inspired . . .

Marcus:

I have dogs, my lord,
Will rouse the proudest panther in the chase,
And climb the highest promontory top.

Titus Andronicus:

And I have horse will follow where the game
Makes way, and run like swallows o'er the plain.

Demetrius:

Chiron, we hunt not, we, with horse nor hound;
But hope to pluck a dainty doe to ground.

THE PEACOCK

TROILUS AND CRESSIDA

ACT III   SCENE III

Thersites:

Why, he stalks up and down like a peacock, – a stride, and a stand: ruminates, like an hostess that hath no arithmetic but her brain to set down her reckoning: bites his lip with a politic regard, as who would say, – *there were wit in this head, an't would out*; and so there is; but it lies as coldly in him as fire in a flint, which will not show without knocking. The man's undone for ever; for if Hector break not his neck i' the combat, he'll break it himself in vain-glory. He knows not me: I said, *Good morrow, Ajax*; and he replies, *Thanks, Agamemnon*. What think you of this man, that takes me for the general? He is grown a very land-fish, languageless, a monster. A plague of opinion! a man may wear it on both sides, like a leather jerkin.

THE RABBIT

LOVE'S LABOUR'S LOST

ACT III   SCENE I

Moth:

Master, will you win your love with a French brawl?

Armado:

How meanest thou? brawling in French?

Moth:

No, my complete master: but to jig off a tune at the tongue's end, canary to it with your feet, humour it with turning up your eyelids; sigh a note, and sing a note; sometime through the throat, as if you swallowed love with singing love; sometime through the nose, as if you snuffed up love by smelling love; with your hat, penthouse-like, o'er the shop of your eyes; with your arms crossed on your thin belly-doublet, like a rabbit on a spit; or your hands in your pocket, like a man after the old painting; and keep not too long in one tune, but a snip and away. These are complements, these are humours; these betray nice wenches, that would be betrayed without these; and make them men of note, (do you note, men?) that most are affected to these.

THE RAM

THE MERCHANT OF VENICE

ACT I   SCENE III

Shylock:

When Jacob grazed his uncle Laban's sheep,
This Jacob from our holy Abraham was
(As his wise mother wrought in his behalf)
The third possessor; ay, he was the third.

Antonio:

And what of him? did he take interest?

Shylock:

No, not take interest; not, as you would say,
Directly interest: mark what Jacob did.
When Laban and himself were compromised,
That all the eanlings which were streak'd and pied
Should fall, as Jacob's hire; the ewes, being rank,
In end of autumn turned to the rams:
And when the work of generation was
Between these woolly breeders in the act,
The skilful shepherd pill'd me certain wands,
And, in the doing of the deed of kind,
He stuck them up before the fulsome ewes;
Who, then conceiving, did in eaning-time
Fall particolour'd lambs, and those were Jacob's.
This was a way to thrive, and he was blest;
And thrift is blessing, if men steal it not.

THE RAM

AS YOU LIKE IT

ACT III   SCENE II

Corin:

Sir, I am a true labourer; I earn that I eat, get that I wear; owe no man hate, envy no man's happiness; glad of other men's good, content with my harm; and the greatest of my pride is, to see my ewes graze and my lambs suck.

Touchstone:

That is another simple sin in you; to bring the ewes and the rams together, and to offer to get your living by the copulation of cattle: to be bawd to a bell-wether; and to betray a she-lamb of a twelvemonth, to a crooked-pated, old, cuckoldly ram, out of all reasonable match. If thou be'st not damned for this, the devil himself will have no shepherds; I cannot see else how thou shouldst 'scape.

HE RAT

THE MERCHANT OF VENICE

ACT IV   SCENE I

Shylock:

What if my house be troubled with a rat,
And I be pleased to give ten thousand ducats
To have it baned? What, are you answer'd yet?
Some men there are love not a gaping pig;
Some, that are mad if they behold a cat;
And others, when the bagpipe sings i' the nose,
Cannot contain their urine: for affection,
Master of passion, sways it to the mood
Of what it likes, or loathes. Now, for your
    answer.
As there is no firm reason to be render'd,
Why he cannot abide a gaping pig;
Why he, a harmless necessary cat;
Why he, a woollen bagpipe, – but of force
Must yield to such inevitable shame,
As to offend, himself being offended;
So can I give no reason, nor I will not,
More than a lodged hate, and a certain loathing,
I bear Antonio, that I follow thus
A losing suit against him.

THE STAG

ACT IV   SCENE II

French General:

Hark! hark! the Dauphin's drum, a warning bell,
Sings heavy music to thy timorous soul,
And mine shall ring thy dire departure out.

Talbot:

He fables not, I hear the enemy; –
Out, some light horsemen, and peruse their wings. –
O, negligent and heedless discipline!
How are we park'd, and bounded in a pale;
A little herd of England's timorous deer,
Mazed with a yelping kennel of French curs!
If we be English deer, be then in blood:
Not rascal-like, to fall down with a pinch;
But rather moody-mad and desperate stags,
Turn on the bloody hounds with heads of steel,
And make the cowards stand aloof at bay:
Sell every man his life as dear as mine,
And they shall find dear deer of us, my friends.
God, and saint George! Talbot, and England's right!
Prosper our colours in this dangerous fight!

THE STAG

ACT V   SCENE V

Falstaff:

The Windsor bell hath struck twelve; the minute draws on: now the hot-blooded gods assist me! – Remember, Jove, thou wast a bull for thy Europa; love set on thy horns. O powerful love! that, in some respects, makes a beast a man; in some other, a man a beast. You were also, Jupiter, a swan, for the love of Leda: – O, omni-potent love! how near the god drew to the complexion

of a goose! – A fault done first in the form of a beast; –
O Jove, a beastly fault! and then another fault in the
semblance of a fowl! think on't, Jove; a foul fault.
When gods have hot backs, what shall poor men do?
For me, I am here a Windsor stag; and the fattest, I
think, i' the forest: send me a cool rut-time, Jove, or
who can blame me to piss my tallow? Who comes
here? my doe?

Mistress Ford:

Sir John? art thou there, my deer? my male deer?

Falstaff:

My doe with the black scut. Let the sky rain potatoes;
let it thunder to the tune of *Green Sleeves*; hail kissing-
comfits, and snow eringoes; let there come a tempest
of provocation, I will shelter me here.

Mistress Ford:

Mistress Page is come with me, sweetheart.

Falstaff:

Divide me like a bribe-buck, each a haunch: I will keep
my sides to myself, my shoulders for the fellow of this
walk, and my horns I bequeath your husbands. Am I a
woodman? ha! Speak I like Herne the hunter? – Why,
now is Cupid a child of conscience: he makes rest-
itution. As I am a true spirit, welcome!

THE TIGER

THE TWO GENTLEMEN OF VERONA

ACT III   SCENE II

Proteus:

S ay, that upon the altar of her beauty
You sacrifice your tears, your sighs, your heart:
Write till your ink be dry; and with your tears
Moist it again; and frame some feeling line,
That may discover such integrity:
For Orpheus' lute was strung with poets' sinews;
Whose golden touch could soften steel and stones,
Make tigers tame, and huge leviathans
Forsake unsounded deeps to dance on sands.
After your dire lamenting elegies,
Visit by night your lady's chamber-window,
With some sweet consort: to their instruments
Tune a deploring dump; the night's dead silence
Will well become such sweet complaining grievance.
This or else nothing, will inherit her.

Duke:

This discipline shows thou hast been in love.

Thurio:

And thy advice this night I'll put in practice.
Therefore, sweet Proteus, my direction-giver,
Let us into the city presently
To sort some gentlemen well-skill'd in music:
I have a sonnet that will serve the turn,
To give the onset to thy good advice.

THE TIGER

ACT IV   SCENE II

Albany:

Wisdom and goodness to the vile seem vile:
Filths savour but themselves. What have you
    done:
Tigers, not daughters, what have you perform'd?
A father, and a gracious agèd man,
Whose reverence even the head-lugg'd bear
    would lick, –
Most barbarous, most degenerate! – have you
    madded.
Could my good brother suffer you to do it?
A man, a prince, by him so benefited?
If that the heavens do not their visible spirits
Send quickly down to tame these vile offences,
'Twill come,
Humanity must perforce prey on itself,
Like monsters of the deep.

59

THE TOAD

TIMON OF ATHENS

ACT IV   SCENE III

Timon:

That nature, being sick of man's unkindness,
Should yet be hungry! – Common mother, thou,
Whose womb unmeasurable, and infinite breast,
Teems, and feeds all; whose self-same mettle,
Whereof thy proud child, arrogant man, is puff'd,
Engenders the black toad, and adder blue,
The gilded newt, and eyeless venom'd worm,
With all the abhorred births below crisp heaven
Whereon Hyperion's quickening fire doth shine;
Yield him, who all the human sons doth hate,
From forth thy plenteous bosom, one poor root!
Ensear thy fertile and conceptious womb,
Let it no more bring out ingrateful man!
Go great with tigers, dragons, wolves, and bears;
Teem with new monsters, whom thy upward face
Hath to the marbled mansion all above
Never presented! – O, a root, – dear thanks!
Dry up thy marrows, vines, and plough-torn leas;
Whereof ingrateful man, with liquorish draughts,
And morsels unctuous, greases his pure mind,
That from it all consideration slips!

THE TOAD

ACT II   SCENE I

Duke:

Sweet are the uses of adversity;
Which, like the toad, ugly and venomous,
Wears yet a precious jewel in his head;
And this our life, exempt from public haunt,
Finds tongues in trees, books in the running brooks,
Sermons in stones, and good in everything.
I would not change it.

Amiens:

Happy is your grace,
That can translate the stubbornness of fortune
Into so quiet and so sweet a style.

$\mathcal{T}$HE UNICORN

THE TEMPEST

ACT III   SCENE III

Sebastian:

Now I will believe
That there are unicorns; that in Arabia
There is one tree, the phoenix' throne; one phoenix
At this hour reigning there.

Antonio:

I'll believe both:
And what does else want credit, come to me,
And I'll be sworn 'tis true. Travellers ne'er did lie,
Though fools at home condemn them.

Gonzalo:

If in Naples
I should report this now, would they believe me?
If I should say I saw such islanders,
(For, certes, these are people of the island,)
Who, though they are of monstrous shape, yet,
     note,
Their manners are more gentle-kind, than of
Our human generation you shall find
Many, nay, almost any.

THE UNICORN

JULIUS CAESAR

ACT II   SCENE I

Decius:

Never fear that: if he be so resolved,
I can o'ersway him: for he loves to hear
That unicorns may be betray'd with trees,
And bears with glasses, elephants with holes,
Lions with toils, and men with flatterers:
But when I tell him he hates flatterers,
He says he does; being then most flatter'd.

Picture Credits

The animal illustrations (except for those on pp. 6, 7 and 10, from the Mary Evans Picture Library) are taken from MS Ashmole 1504, reproduced by courtesy of the Bodleian Library, Oxford. Folio numbers, from which the details are taken, are listed after the page numbers:

p.1: f.39; p.2T (top): f.3lv, B (bottom): f.34; p.3: f.37v; p.5: f.4l; p.13: f.30; p.l5: f.3l; p.16: f.41; p.l7: f.37; p.l8: f.32v; p.21: f.38v; p.22: f.37; p.24: f.33v; p.25: f.34v; p.27: f.34v; p.29: f.40v; p.30: f.39v: p.31T: f.33, B: f.38v; p.32T: f.30v, B: f.35; p.33: f.35; p.35T: f.34, B: f.30v; p.36T: f.37v, B: 33v; p.38: f.32; p.39: f.35; p.40: f.37; p.4l: f.36v; p.44T: f.36, B: f.30; p.45: f.35v; p46: f.39; p.48: f.36; p.50: f.40; p.52: f.4l; p.54: f.4lv; p.56: f.38; p.59: f.4l; p.60: f.32; p.61: f.4lv; p.63: f.37v